Business and Technology

Lee Coutts and **Alistair Wylie**

CfE
Curriculum for Excellence

HODDER
GIBSON
AN HACHETTE UK COMPANY

CW01460633

Acknowledgements

The Publishers would like to thank the following for permission to reproduce copyright material:

Photo credits

p.viii (from top) © Natasha Japp/iStockphoto.com, © GPI/Alamy, © InsideOutPix/Alamy, © BasieB/iStockphoto.com, © Andrey Prokhorov/iStockphoto.com; p.5 © Lee Coutts; p.14 (left) © JackF/Fotolia.com, (right) © Juanmonino/iStockphoto.com; p.20 © Andrey Prokhorov/iStockphoto.com; p.33 © Timothy Large/Alamy; p.39 © Child Expolitation & Online Protection (www.clickceop.net); p.40 (from top) © pizuttipics/Fotolia.com, © Dmitriy Chistoprudov/Fotolia.com, © Reinhold Föger/Fotolia.com, © yobidaba/Fotolia.com; p.41 (from top) © Twitter Inc., © Wikipedia, © digitallife/Alamy, © Vladislav Kochelaevskiy/Alamy; p.46 (from top) © Konstantin Shevtsov – Fotolia, © JackF – Fotolia, © Dragan Radojkovic - Fotolia.com, © slobo/istockphoto; p.47 (from top) © pizuttipics – Fotolia, © Yuri Arcurs – Fotolia.

Every effort has been made to trace all copyright holders, but if any have been inadvertently overlooked the Publishers will be pleased to make the necessary arrangements at the first opportunity.

Although every effort has been made to ensure that website addresses are correct at time of going to press, Hodder Gibson cannot be held responsible for the content of any website mentioned in this book. It is sometimes possible to find a relocated web page by typing in the address of the home page for a website in the URL window of your browser.

Hachette UK's policy is to use papers that are natural, renewable and recyclable products and made from wood grown in sustainable forests. The logging and manufacturing processes are expected to conform to the environmental regulations of the country of origin.

Orders: please contact Bookpoint Ltd, 130 Milton Park, Abingdon, Oxon OX14 4SB. Telephone: (44) 01235 827720. Fax: (44) 01235 400454. Lines are open 9.00–5.00, Monday to Saturday, with a 24-hour message answering service. Visit our website at www.hoddereducation.co.uk. Hodder Gibson can be contacted direct on: Tel: 0141 848 1609; Fax: 0141 889 6315; email: hoddergibson@hodder.co.uk

© Lee Coutts and Alistair Wylie 2012
First published in 2012 by
Hodder Gibson, an imprint of Hodder Education,
An Hachette UK Company
2a Christie Street
Paisley PA1 1NB

Impression number   5 4 3 2 1
Year   2015 2014 2013 2012

All rights reserved. Apart from any use permitted under UK copyright law, no part of this publication may be reproduced or transmitted in any form or by any means, electronic or mechanical, including photocopying and recording, or held within any information storage and retrieval system, without permission in writing from the publisher or under licence from the Copyright Licensing Agency Limited. Further details of such licences (for reprographic reproduction) may be obtained from the Copyright Licensing Agency Limited, Saffron House, 6–10 Kirby Street, London EC1N 8TS.

Cover photo © moodboard / Fotolia.com
Illustrations by Emma Golley at Redmoor Design, Jeff Edwards and DC Graphic Design Limited, Swanley, Kent
Typeset in Myriad Pro Light 10/13.5pt by DC Graphic Design Limited, Swanley, Kent
Printed in Italy

A catalogue record for this title is available from the British Library
ISBN: 978 1444 158 663

Contents

Introduction

Welcome to Curriculum for Excellence (CfE) for Business and Technology level 3.

This book has been written to support the new experiences and outcomes of Curriculum for Excellence. In particular, it focuses on the level 3 outcomes relating to Business Education. These are mainly to be found as part of the Social Studies experiences and outcomes and Technologies experiences and outcomes. Opportunities for the development of outcomes in Literacy, Numeracy and Health and Wellbeing have also been included where appropriate.

This book assumes that learners have completed the relevant Social Studies and Technologies experiences and outcomes at level 2.

How to use this book

This book is based around a scenario – Huntingdale Garden Centre. This is a fictional scenario but is one which presents situations that should be familiar to learners. All learning and activities evolve from the central scenario and are divided into Integrated Learning Objects (ILOs). Integrated Learning Objects are the authors' interpretation of one way in which to deliver an integrated educational solution to the delivery of experiences and outcomes as part of a scenario. Each ILO includes knowledge notes, revision activities and explanations of terms. Most importantly, each ILO is built around a further development of the original scenario provided at the start of the book. Each ILO can be carried out individually or as a group.

The book integrates the experiences and outcomes and does not need to be delivered in a sequential order. ILOs are mainly drawn from the Social Studies outcomes although there is also reference to some of the Technologies outcomes. Whilst there is a connection to Business, the Technologies outcomes are more closely related to the new subject area of Administration and IT. However, technology and the use of IT are central to teaching and learning and this is recognised in the tasks that have been set. There are also strong links to Literacy and Numeracy and opportunities throughout the book to develop good written and oral communication skills.

This book should be viewed as a starting point for further learning, teaching and development and should not be viewed as a definitive source or a textbook to be used as a template for a course at this level. This would not support the ethos of Curriculum for Excellence.

A matrix of the experiences and outcomes mapped to ILOs in the book has been provided.

It is envisaged that teachers will adapt, develop and change tasks to suit their own needs and those of their learners. Again, these tasks should not be seen as definitive in nature or content. It would be possible to write further ILOs based on the background scenario provided or to build on the scenario or further extend the ILOs in the book.

A selection of e-files to accompany the Tasks in the book are available to download free of charge from www.hoddereducation.co.uk/CfEBusiness. The CustomerDatabase file has been supplied as an Excel spreadsheet which can be easily imported into your preferred database software. You should do this prior to making the file available to your students. The contents of the e-files are also reproduced in the Appendices.

About the authors

Lee Coutts and **Alistair Wylie** are experienced authors and educators in Business Education. Both have taught in the secondary and further education sectors and have experience of working in the national education arena. They have both published a wide variety of texts individually. This text is their second joint publication.

Dedications

For Aidan, a constant support and inspiration.

Huntingdale Garden Centre background information

Alice and Lee Huntingdale live in North Berwick where they attend the local school. North Berwick is a seaside town about 35km to the east of Edinburgh. Alice and Lee's parents, Tom and Lisa, own and run the Huntingdale Garden Centre which is located on the outskirts of the town. It is a family-owned business and one of the largest garden centres in the area.

This year is a special year as the garden centre has been open for 15 years. Tom and Lisa have special events planned to celebrate the 15 years that they have been in business as a partnership. They are a partnership because there are two of them in charge of the business. If there had been just one of them running the business, it would have been a sole trader.

Huntingdale Garden Centre stocks a wide range of products including the following:

- plants

- flowers

- homeware

- food and drink

- garden furniture

- hot tubs

- greenhouses

- café.

The garden centre is a well-known feature of the local community. Most of its customers live locally and visit the garden centre regularly. Special events are often arranged and the garden centre offers a series of regular guest speakers. The guest speakers are often well-known gardeners, sometimes from the local area and sometimes from further afield. Recently, a celebrity gardener visited Huntingdale Garden Centre to give a talk. This was very good for business.

Huntingdale Garden Centre is keen to support the environment. It has an environmental policy which aims to make the business as 'green' as possible. It encourages all of its customers to recycle. To support this, it has a large recycling station at the garden centre where customers can recycle everything from batteries to carrier bags and bottles. It also offers for sale its own range of organic products for the organic gardener. This includes soil, compost and insecticides.

When they are not at school, Alice and Lee help their parents by working in the garden centre. They often get asked to carry out lots of different tasks and this is something that they enjoy. Sometimes they work alone, sometimes they work together as a team and sometimes they work with their parents.

Plans are well under way to celebrate the 15th birthday of the opening of the garden centre. Tom and Lisa are planning a party to be held on 5 June as well as the activities listed in the table below throughout the year:

Month	Activity/Offer
January	10% off all winter plants
February	15% off all seeds for spring sowing
March	10% off all garden tools
April	10% off tubs and planters
May	15% off summer plants and flowers
June	FREE entry into a prize draw to win £1000 cash with every purchase made during this month. The more you buy the more times you will be entered!
July	10% off grass seeds and grass care products
August	15% off all garden machines (excluding petrol models)
September	20% off compost, fertiliser and bark
October	10% off all garden recycling products
November	10% off jams and preserves
December	10% off Christmas decorations

The special birthday at Huntingdale Garden Centre on 5 June is to be marked by an open day with various activities throughout the site including:

- face painting
- bouncy castle
- guest speakers
- ice carving
- free food and drinks
- free ice creams
- firework display at dusk.

Tom and Lisa are inviting special guests from the local community including the Mayor, the local radio station DJ and children from the local primary school.

There is also a free prize draw for all who come along on the day. There are three prizes on offer. First prize is a £1000 voucher to spend in the garden centre. Second prize is a £500 voucher and third prize is a £250 voucher. The prize draw is free to enter. Visitors can pick up a ticket on the day at the garden centre and the prize draw will take place at the end of the day.

Check your learning

1 Where is Huntingdale Garden Centre located?

Tick the correct box.	
Glasgow	
North Berwick	
Dundee	
Aberdeen	

2 List two products that Huntingdale Garden Centre sells.

3 What type of business do Tom and Lisa run?

Tick the correct box.	
Sole trader	
Partnership	

4 Give an advantage of the type of business they run.

5 Give a disadvantage of the type of business they run.

6 Name two things that Huntingdale Garden Centre does to be 'green'.

7 Huntingdale Garden Centre has been open for a long time. What birthday is it about to celebrate?

8 What discount would you get if you bought the following products in the month given? Fill in the table.

	Discount
Winter plants in January	
Garden tools in February	
Grass seed in July	
Compost in September	
Jams in November	
Christmas decorations in December	

9 Alistair spent £50.00 on Christmas decorations in December.
   a) Calculate how much discount he would get.
   b) Calculate how much money he would have to pay Huntingdale Garden Centre.

10 Katie spent £30.00 on preserves in November.
   a) Calculate how much discount she would get.
   b) Calculate how much money she would have to pay Huntingdale Garden Centre.

11 Aidan bought a number of things in March. He had to pay Huntingdale Garden Centre a total of £60.00. He knew he got 10% off the garden tools he bought (which before discount came to £44.00), but he wasn't sure how much it cost him for the compost he also bought.
   a) How much discount (in £) would he get on the garden tools?
   b) How much did it cost him for the compost?

12 When is the open day for Huntingdale Garden Centre's birthday?

13 Name two attractions that will be at the open day.

14 What prize do you get if you come first in the prize draw?

15 Do you have to pay to take part in the prize draw?

Furniture
Hot Tubs
Greenhouses

Café

Garden
Centre

Outdoor Plant
Area

The
"Wilderness"

Car Park
Extension

Car Park

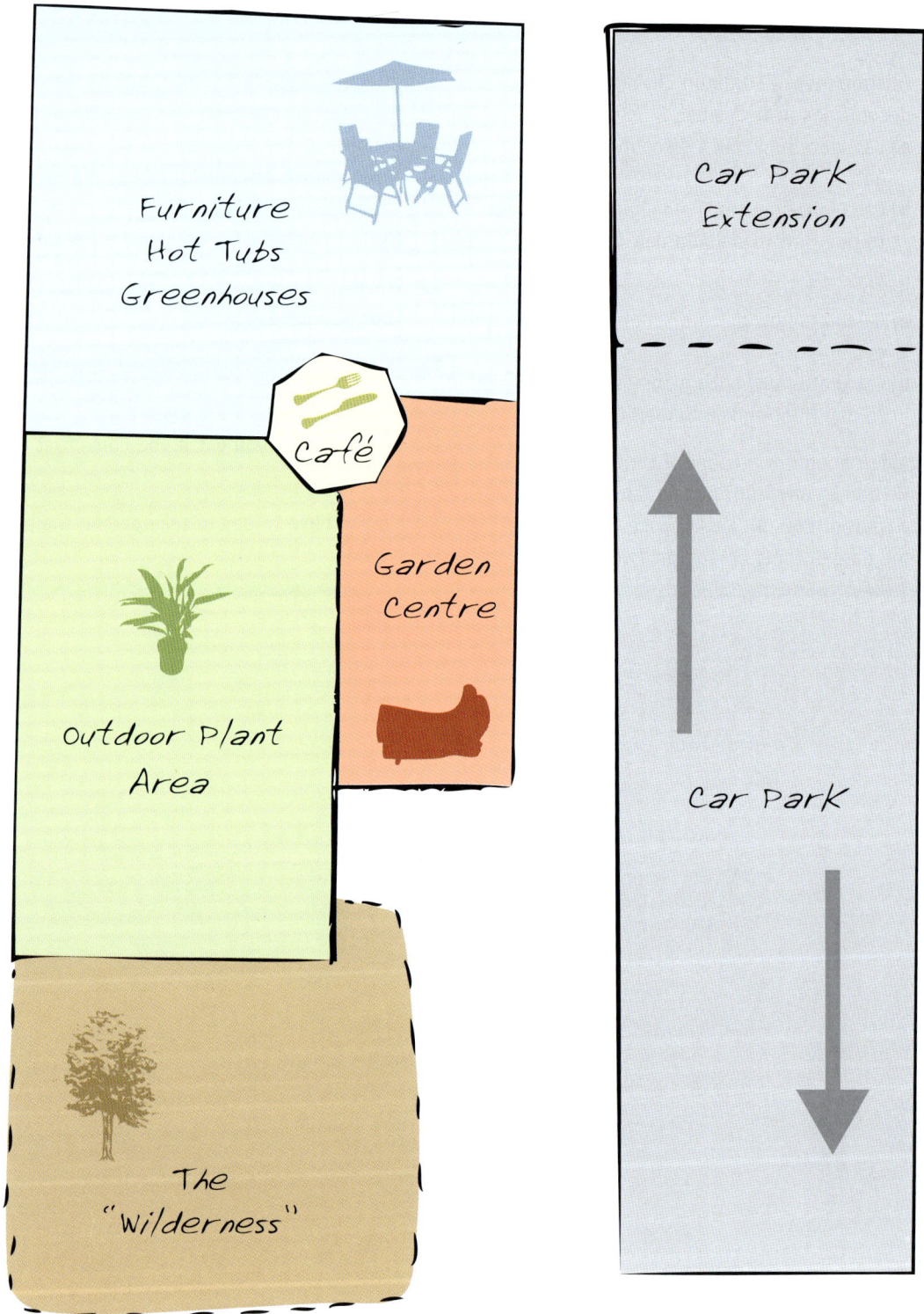

Map of Huntingdale Garden Centre

Why business? Why here?

Experiences and outcomes covered	SOC 3–11a, TCH 3–04a, TCH 3–07b
Topics covered	Social and economic costs and benefits, business location
Knowledge and skills	Research, creative thought, word processing
Resources needed	Access to the Internet, word-processing software, digital camera or mobile phone with camera

What this means

Benefits these are advantages.

Costs these are disadvantages.

Huntingdale Garden Centre is located on the outskirts of North Berwick. As well as offering a number of different products for sale, the Garden Centre brings a number of **benefits** and **costs** to North Berwick.

The location of Huntingdale Garden Centre

Jobs for people

Recycling facilities for the community

Choice for customers

Benefits to North Berwick

Events for the local community

Competition for other businesses (might mean better prices)

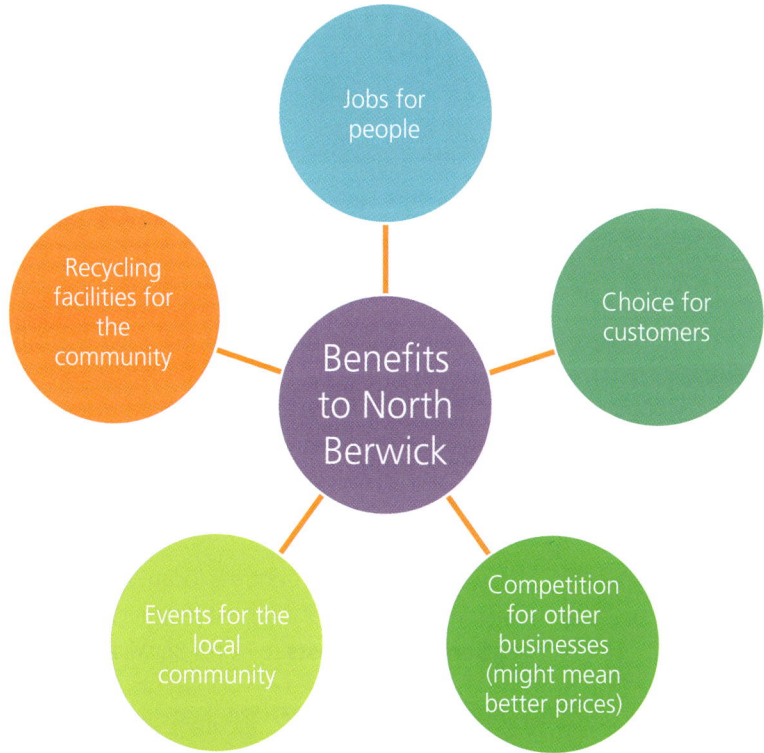

However, there are also costs:

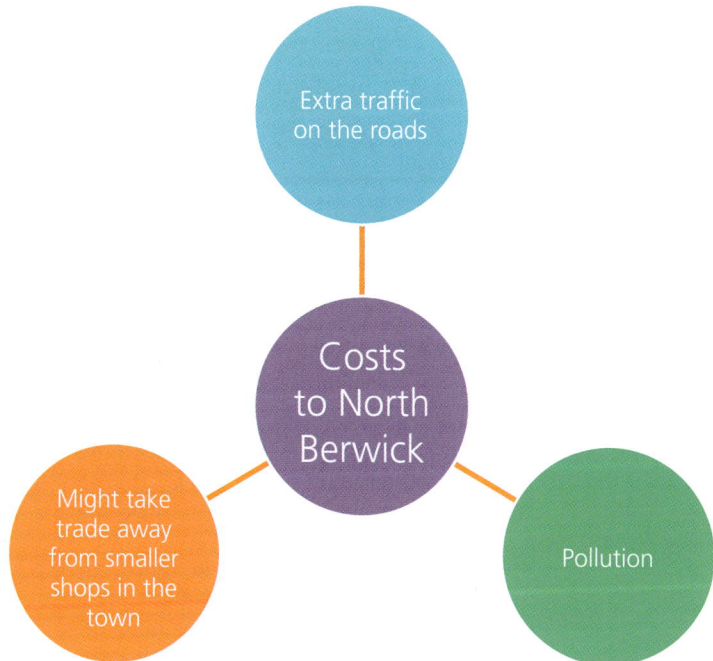

Extra traffic on the roads

Costs to North Berwick

Might take trade away from smaller shops in the town

Pollution

When a new business opens in any location, it has a number of different costs and benefits for the local community. Some of these costs and benefits have been given here. However, there are others. Sometimes new roads might have to be created, new schools built and new shops built; sometimes new businesses take customers from existing businesses and therefore these fail.

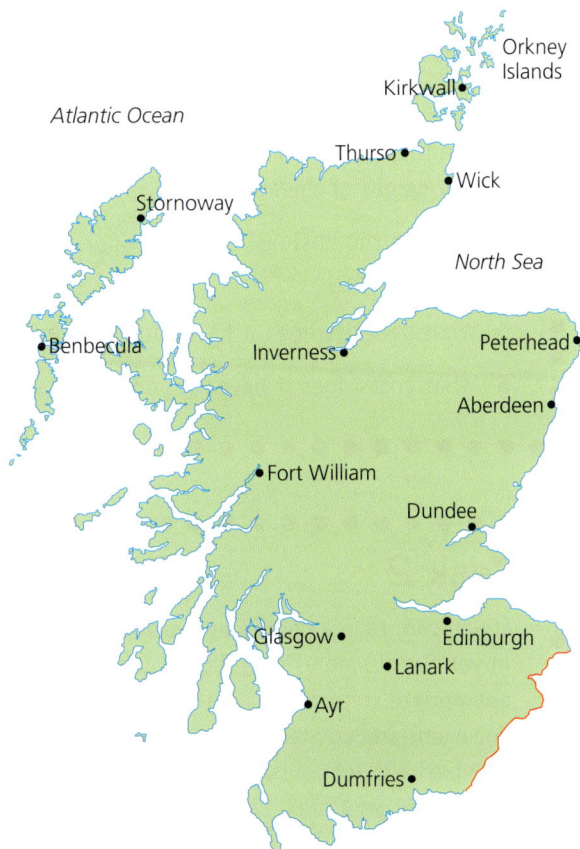

There are lots of things to consider when deciding where to set up a new business

Tom and Lisa Huntingdale will have thought very carefully about where to set up before choosing the location in North Berwick. They would have thought about:

- existing businesses (**competition**) in the area
- whether there was **demand** for their products
- whether they were close to a supplier
- whether there was access by road to their chosen location
- whether there was enough car parking space in their chosen location
- whether there was access to running water and electricity in their chosen location
- the Internet and **broadband** speed available.

What this means

Competition a business that offers the same or similar product to another.

Demand people want to buy a product.

Broadband a special type of Internet connection that is fast.

Task 1

Think about a new business that has opened up in your local area recently and answer the questions given below. You might want to do some Internet research to help you.

1   What is the name of the new business in your area?

2   What does it sell?

3   Are there other similar businesses to this in your area? What are the names of them?

4   Why did the business set up in your area? (Try to think of at least two reasons.)

5   What benefits does it have for your area?

6   What costs does it have for your area?

Task 2

If you can, take a photograph of the new business that opened up in your local area using a digital camera or mobile phone. Using appropriate software, place this photograph into a word-processing document and create a poster showing the benefits and costs of this new business for your area. (If you can't take a photo of the actual business in your area, search the Internet for another suitable photo.)

Carry out a peer assessment of at least two other people's work for Task 2. Complete a Peer Assessment Sheet for each person (your teacher will give you copies). The Sheet can be photocopied from the Appendices.

Task 3

Email the poster you created in Task 2 to your teacher or to a parent/carer to show them what you have been learning about in Business!

Remember, if you are sending an email there are some rules to follow.

- Key in the receiver's email address carefully.
- Include a subject heading (this is important so that the receiver knows what the email is about).
- Write in proper English (not text language!)
- Write your name at the end of the email so that the receiver knows who it is from.
- Remember to attach your file before clicking 'Send'.

Task 4

Read the following newspaper article and answer the question that follows.

Tom Huntingdale was reading the newspaper one Sunday and noticed the advert shown below. He began to think that opening a garden centre in this area of Glasgow might be a good idea. Why might he have thought this? Try to find at least three reasons.

New Developments in Glasgow

Glasgow Harbour is one of Glasgow's newest housing developments. It offers the luxury of living like a VIP in a quiet area, surrounded by stunning views of the River Clyde.

Surrounded by unoccupied land, Glasgow Harbour offers luxury living for hundreds of people. Just off the main motorway running through Glasgow, it is easy to get to and only a few minutes' walk from Partick railway station. Furthermore, the Glasgow Riverside Museum, Glasgow Science Centre, The Scottish Hydro Arena and the SECC are its neighbours.

Why business? Why here?

What this means

Benefits these are advantages.

Broadband a special type of Internet connection that is fast.

Competition a business that offers the same or similar product to another.

Costs these are disadvantages.

Demand people want to buy a product.

Links to other subjects

In Geography/Environmental Studies you might learn about the impact business and industry can have on the local environment.

In Administration and IT you will learn about sending emails with attachments, including the rules for sending emails.

Check your learning

1 Why might the Huntingdale Garden Centre have set up in North Berwick?

Tick all the correct answers.	
Close to suppliers	
Lots of customers	
No electricity	
No car parking space	
No other similar businesses	

2 Huntingdale Garden Centre is located on the outskirts of North Berwick. Decide if each of the following factors is a benefit or cost to North Berwick.

	Benefit or cost?
Increased pollution	
More jobs	
Events for the local community	
Cheaper prices for customers	
Extra traffic on roads	
More recycling facilities	

3 What recycling facilities does Huntingdale Garden Centre have for its customers? (You might need to look back at the background information if you can't remember!)

4 What is the difference between a cost and a benefit?

5 Why does an email have a subject heading?

6 Answer the following questions by writing true or false next to each one.
   a) Huntingdale Garden Centre might bring extra tourism to North Berwick.
   b) Being able to include an attachment in an email is an advantage of using email.
   c) Competition sometimes means that customers get cheaper prices.
   d) A business won't locate in a certain place if there is no demand for the product in that area.
   e) Access to running water and electricity is important when choosing a new business location.
   f) A reliable and fast broadband connection is important for business.

How much? Can we afford this?

Experiences and outcomes covered	SOC 3–21a, TCH 3–06a, TCH 3–07b, MNU 3–09b
Topics covered	Finance, budgeting, advertising/marketing/presentation
Knowledge and skills	Word processing, spreadsheets, charts, numeracy, creative thought
Resources needed	Access to a computer, word-processing software, spreadsheet software, relevant e-files (see Introduction)

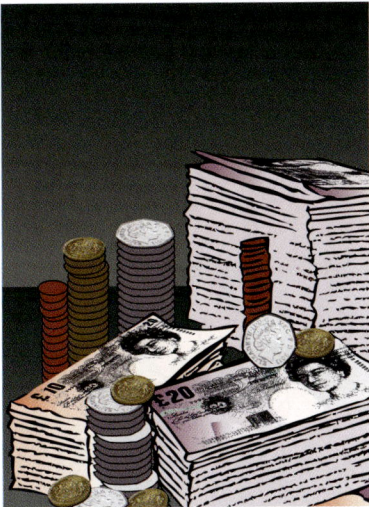

It is said that money makes the world go round. Think, for a moment, about how you would manage to live if you did not have any money.

In a small group, or individually, think about the work that your parents or carers carry out. How do they spend the money that they earn? Make a list of things that you and your family need money for. Discuss this if you are in a group.

In business, money is needed for many different things. The things that need to be paid are often called **expenses**. Here are some examples:

- Paying the workers.
- Paying the gas, electricity and telephone bills.
- Paying for things to help grow the business.
- Paying for new premises.
- Paying for new equipment.

Most people who are in business like to make money. They call the money that they make '**profit**'. Sometimes they may be able to use some of their profit to help grow the business. This could be done by buying larger premises or by hiring more staff. Sometimes, however, a business wants to grow but does not have the money or profits to do so. When this happens, the owners of the business might consider borrowing the money from someone else.

Can you think of people or places that a business could borrow money from?

The most common sources of money that is borrowed in business are:

- **Overdraft** – this is where the bank allows the business to borrow money up to an agreed amount from their existing bank account but only for a short period of time. This is useful for relatively small amounts of money that only need to be borrowed for a short time. The charges for this service are usually quite high.

- **Trade credit** – this is where one business buys goods or services from another business and agrees to pay for them at a later date. Most businesses offer this service to each other. There is no charge as long as the bill is settled within the time period agreed for payment.

- **Hire purchase** – this is often used to buy new equipment. The business pays a fixed amount every month for a period of time. At the end of the 'hire' period, the business will own the equipment.

- **Bank loan** – this is where the business borrows an agreed amount of money from the bank and agrees to pay it back over a fixed period of time – usually monthly. The bank adds on a fee for borrowing the money. They call this an interest charge. This means that, for example, if the business borrows £10,000 and agrees to pay it back over a period of 5 years (60 months) then the total that it will repay to the bank might be £12,000 with the interest added on.

How much? Can we afford this?

What this means

Sales money from things that are sold by a business.

Services things that a business offers to its customers.

Alice and Lee have been working with Tom, their dad. It is February and Tom is concerned about the amount of money being generated by the garden centre. Recently, a new garden centre has opened up on the other side of the town. Although it is much smaller and offers fewer **services**, Tom has noticed that the **sales** at Huntingdale have been lower than expected. Tom has already started work on extending the car parking space and he will have to pay £25,000 to the company carrying out the work when it is complete in two months' time. He is concerned that there will not be enough money to pay for this work if sales do not increase.

What this means

Bank loan money borrowed from a bank and paid back over a period of time along with a charge called interest.

Expenses bills that need to be paid in business.

Hire purchase paying money for something over a period of time until you own it.

Overdraft borrowing money for a short time from the bank.

Profit money that people make in business.

Sales money from things that are sold by a business.

Services things that a business offers to its customers.

Trade credit buying goods from another business and paying for them later.

Task 1

Tom has asked Alice and Lee to complete a spreadsheet (HGC Forecast; see page 53) with the information that he has provided in the file HGC Sales (a word-processing file; see page 52). If there is not going to be enough money to pay for the new car park, Lee and Alice will need to make a suggestion as to how their dad can borrow the money to pay the bill. Use the files provided by your teacher to carry out this task for them.

Task 2

Tom has also asked Alice and Lee to produce a suitable chart which will show the sales figures from last year compared to this year. The sales information is in the file HGC Sales (a word-processing file; see page 52). Use the file provided by your teacher to carry out this task for them.

Task 3

Tom has also asked Alice and Lee to think how the garden centre could increase its sales. One idea is to advertise the benefits of shopping at Huntingdale Garden Centre. Tom thinks it would be a good idea for Alice and Lee to produce a poster that he can use for advertising the garden centre. Use the background information at the start of the book to carry out this task for them.

If you carried out Tasks 1, 2 or 3 as part of a group you may also wish to carry out an evaluation. Use the Peer Assessment Sheet provided by your teacher to do this. The Sheet can be photocopied from the Appendices.

Links to other subjects

In Accounting and Financial Awareness, you will learn about money and how to track it and spend it.

Check your learning

1 How might Tom be able to get money to pay for the car park?

Tick all the correct answers.	
Go to the bank	
Decrease sales	
Borrow money from family	
Ask for donations	
Have a sale	

2 How might Tom and Lisa make the garden centre more competitive against the new garden centre that has opened up?

Tick all answers that you agree with.	
Increase prices	
Create more jobs	
Run events for the local community	
Offer special deals for customers	
Have free parking	
Offer more recycling facilities	

3 Think about the shops that you go to. What kind of special offers do you see that make you want to buy things? Discuss this in a group.

4 Why do you think it is important for the garden centre to grow and develop?

5 Apart from making a bigger car park, can you think of anything else that Tom and Lisa could do to make the garden centre more popular with customers?

Getting bigger? Is it 'fair'?

Experiences and outcomes covered	SOC 3–20a, SOC 3–20b, TCH 3–03a, TCH 3–04a TCH 3–06a, TCH 3–07a, TCH 3–07b
Topics covered	Growth, globalisation, world trade, channel of distribution, profit, objectives, Fairtrade, enterprise activity
Knowledge and skills	Team working, numeracy, preparing and interpreting graphical information, problem solving, research
Resources needed	Access to the Internet, materials for enterprise activity (if appropriate), spreadsheet software

Huntingdale Garden Centre is located on the outskirts of North Berwick, about 35 km to the east of Edinburgh.

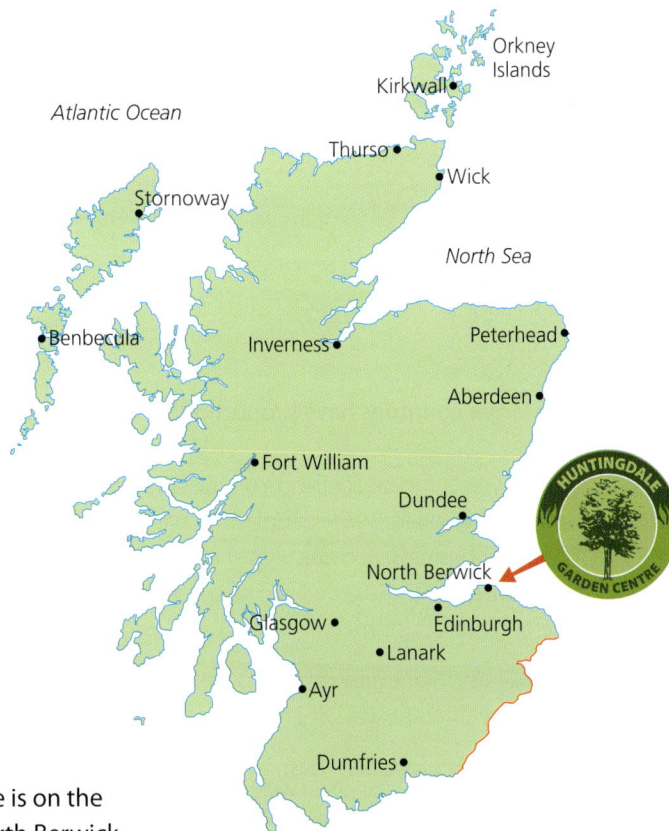

Huntingdale Garden Centre is on the outskirts of the town of North Berwick

Even though Huntingdale Garden Centre is very popular in the area it is based in, compared to the whole of Scotland or the whole world, it is a very small business. Let's compare the **population** of Scotland with that of other countries in the world:

Country	Population
Scotland	5,200,000 people (est. 2010)
Spain	46,196,278 people
Germany	81,796,000 people
United States of America (USA)	313,138,000 people
China	1,347,350,000 people

(Source: Wikipedia http://en.Wikipedia.org/Wiki/List_of_countries_by_population)

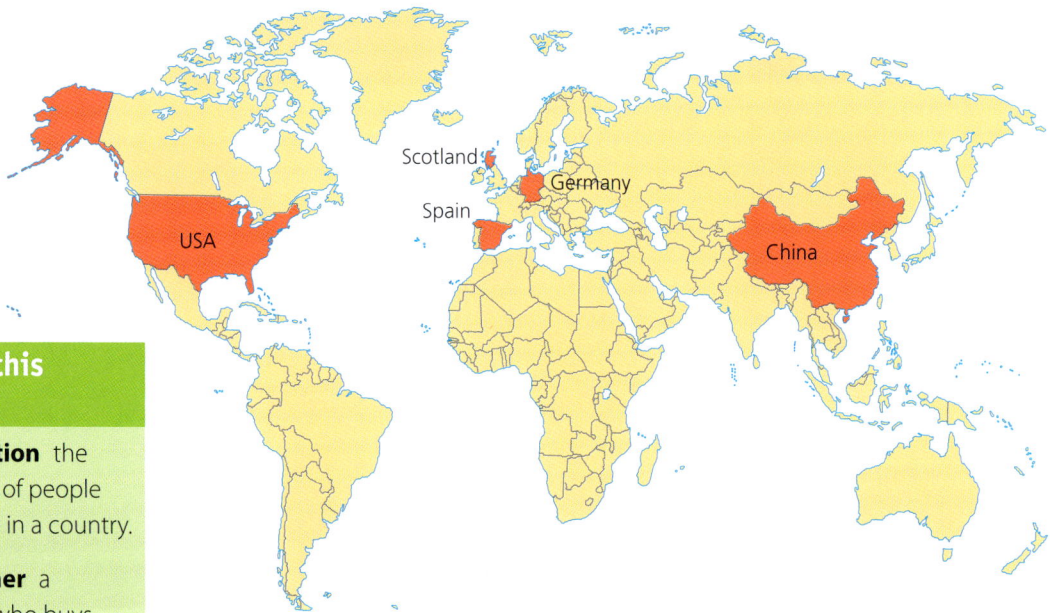

What this means

Population the number of people who live in a country.

Customer a person who buys something from a business.

Profit the money a business makes from selling goods after it has taken off any costs or expenses. Profit = sales – expenses.

Grow to get bigger.

Do larger countries have proportionally larger populations?

When you compare Scotland's population with other countries, it is very small. This might be good for some people who live here because it's quieter, but it isn't always good for business. Because Scotland is smaller, it can be harder to gain more **customers** without growing. The bigger the country, the more chance there is of getting more customers.

A business might grow in size to get more customers (and more **profit**) and can **grow** in different ways. It could:

- sell new products it hasn't sold before
- build an extension onto its shop so that it is bigger

- open up a new shop in another town
- open up a new shop in another country.

When a business opens a new shop or factory in another country, this is known as **globalisation**. Huntingdale Garden Centre could decide to open up a new garden centre in another country so that it can gain more customers and make more profit.

What this means

Globalisation getting bigger by opening a new shop or factory in another country.

Business is good for a country. Without business, people would not have a choice of products to buy and people would be without jobs. When people are without jobs, this means they have less money to spend and therefore cannot afford to buy as many products.

Businesses provide products

↓

These products are bought by customers

↓

The business needs people to work for them to be able to provide products

↓

People who work for a business get money for their work

↓

This money is then used to buy products from other businesses

What this means

Supplier a business that provides products to another business who then sells them to customers.

Different countries rely on businesses in other countries because not every country could produce every product. For example, Scotland can't produce bananas because they won't grow here so we have to buy them from another country.

Sometimes businesses that grow try to make as much profit as possible, by paying less for the products they need to sell. All businesses have **suppliers** that they buy products from and the business then sells these products on to customers:

A farm might grow plants that they will sell to Huntington Garden Centre.	Huntington Garden Centre buys the plants from the supplier and sells these on to customers.	Customers pay money to buy the plants from Huntington Garden Centre.

Huntington Garden Centre sells the plants to its customers at a higher price than it paid its supplier for them. This is because Tom and Lisa want the garden centre to make a profit. **Remember: profit = sales – expenses.**

For example:

- the supplier charges 50p per plant
- Huntington Garden Centre charges 80p per plant
- this means it will make 30p profit per plant sold.

Because businesses think about profit, they want to pay as little as possible to their supplier so that they can make as much profit as possible. However, this might not be a very high price and sometimes the supplier does not get enough money even to cover the cost of making the product.

In countries where there is not much money, some businesses might try to take advantage of this and not treat suppliers very well. The Fairtrade Foundation is working to make sure suppliers get paid a fair amount of money for the products that they make, and ensure that they are treated fairly.

Getting bigger? Is it 'fair'?

What this means

Fairtrade making sure suppliers get a fair price for their products and are treated fairly.

You will see examples of the **Fairtrade** logo on different products in supermarkets, and this shows customers that the product has been produced in a way that is fair to the business that made it.

Task 1

Create a graph using the figures given in the population table on page 12. Make sure you label your graph with a title and, where appropriate, label each axis. If you can, you might want to create your graph using a spreadsheet package.

Task 2

Scotland has a population of 5.2 million people. Its capital city is Edinburgh and it is known across the world for producing whisky and shortbread.

Choose a country and do some Internet research to find out:

- the population of the country
- the capital city of the country
- what products are produced in the country.

Once you have done your research, ask your teacher to tell you how you should present this. You might be able to put your information into a wiki or blog so that other people in your class can read it. (See page 41 for more information on what these are.)

Task 3

The Fairtrade Foundation is responsible for making sure products with the Fairtrade logo have been produced in a fair way. Visit their website **www.fairtrade.org.uk** to find out more about Fairtrade.

Your teacher might ask you to look at certain pages on this website to find out more about different products, to meet some of the farmers or to find out some facts and figures about Fairtrade.

Getting bigger? Is it 'fair'?

Task 4

You have been asked to work out how much profit was made in January on the different products that Huntingdale Garden Centre sold. Open the spreadsheet file HGCProfit (see page 54) and follow the instructions below.

- Format the columns containing price as currency.
- Enter appropriate formulae to calculate the profit made per unit.
- Enter appropriate formulae to calculate the total profit made per product.
- Create a chart that compares the sales of each product.
- Make sure your chart is correctly labelled.

Once you have carried out the above tasks, answer the following questions.

1 What was the total profit made?

2 Which product sold most units?

3 Which product sold least units?

4 Which product made most profit?

5 Which product made least profit?

You may have carried out Task 4 as part of a group. If so, now complete the Peer Assessment Sheet which will be provided by your teacher. The Sheet can be photocopied from the Appendices.

Task 5

This task is designed to be completed as a class or group activity.

You are going to run a Fairtrade tuck shop in your school. The tuck shop could be open during one break time, lunchtime or even during a school event (e.g. disco or open evening) and will give everyone in your school the opportunity to learn about Fairtrade and to buy a Fairtrade product. You could sell Fairtrade fruit, chocolate, juice and soap – these are just some examples.

Your teacher will help you carry out this task as you will have lots of planning to do to make sure things go well. You need to decide:

- when the tuck shop will be open
- what products you can sell and where to get them
- how much to charge for each Fairtrade product (remember, you want to make a profit – this could go to a Fairtrade charity!)
- how you will record the money you spend on buying products, how many of each item to buy, and what profit you make (you could use a spreadsheet to help)
- how to advertise your tuck shop
- who will carry out different tasks before, during and after the tuck shop.

Once you have carried out your tuck shop task, you should think about what went well, what didn't go well and what you would do differently next time. Use the Peer Assessment sheet provided by your teacher.

What this means

Customer a person who buys something from a business.

Fairtrade making sure suppliers get a fair price and are treated fairly.

Globalisation getting bigger by opening a new shop or factory in another country.

Grow to get bigger.

Population the number of people who live in a country.

Profit the money a business makes from selling goods after it has taken off any costs or expenses. Profit = sales – expenses.

Supplier a business that provides products to another business who then sells them to customers.

Getting bigger? Is it 'fair'?

⚙️ **Links to other subjects**

In Geography you will learn about different countries of the world, the cultures in these countries and how the people of these countries live.

In Maths and numeracy you will learn more about money and how to calculate profit.

In Administration and IT you will learn about using spreadsheets and how to create charts.

Check your learning continued

1 Put these countries in order from the largest population to the smallest:

Spain, China, Scotland, Germany, USA

2 Answer the following questions by writing true or false next to each one.
   a) People might move to Scotland because it's quieter than China.
   b) Businesses would get more customers in Scotland than in Germany.
   c) Businesses would get more customers in China than in Spain.
   d) Businesses can grow by opening up another shop.
   e) Businesses can grow by building a factory in another country.

3 Why might a business like Huntingdale Garden Centre want to grow?

Tick all the correct answers.	
To get more customers	
To make more profit	
To close down	
To get cheaper suppliers	

4 Match each word a–e with the correct description i–v.
   a) supplier
   b) customer
   c) Fairtrade
   d) profit
   e) globalisation

   i) making sure suppliers get treated fairly and get a fair price
   ii) a person who sells a product to another business
   iii) when sales are more than costs a business makes this
   iv) opening up a shop or factory in another country
   v) a person who buys a product from a business

5 Huntingdale Garden Centre wants to sell as many products as possible. Why does it want to do this?

→

6 Huntingdale Garden Centre is not sure which supplier to use for garden furniture. Use the information below to answer the questions given.

	Supplier A cost per item	Supplier B cost per item	Selling price per item
Chair	£5.00	£4.00	£10.00
Table	£20.00	£23.00	£50.00
Umbrella	£8.00	£7.75	£15.00
Chair cushion	£2.00	£2.50	£4.00

a) How much profit would be made on each item if Supplier A was used?

b) How much profit would be made on each item if Supplier B was used?

c) Which supplier should Huntingdale Garden Centre use for each product?

7 Why would a country want a business to locate in their country? Try to think of two reasons.

8 Why do people need jobs? Try to think of two reasons.

9 If you see the Fairtrade logo on a product what does this mean?

10 A spreadsheet was used to create a chart in Task 4. Think of two advantages of using a spreadsheet rather than creating a chart on paper.

How 'green' can we go?

Experiences and outcomes covered	SOC 3–08a, TCH 3–06a, TCH3–07b
Topics covered	Recycling/environmental issues
Knowledge and skills	Word processing, creative thought, research, decision making
Resources needed	Access to a computer, word-processing software

Recycling and **'being green'** are important concepts in our modern society. Are you concerned about the environment? Do you carry out any **recycling** activity at home? Or at school? Make a list of any recycling that you do and discuss and compare this in a group.

In business, it is good practice to have an environmental policy. This means that the business has thought about how the goods and services that it provides impact on the environment. If your business is a supermarket, for example, this could mean that you only provide recycled paper or plastic bags for your customers to use.

The impact that a business has on the environment can be local or further afield. Let's think about the following examples:

1   Which of the following businesses has a greater environmental impact on the local area?

   a) Easyshopper is a local supermarket. It has a lot of cardboard, plastic and packaging that needs to be collected from the store every week. This goes into the normal bin for collection every week.

   b) Happyshopper is another local supermarket. It also has a lot of cardboard, plastic and packaging that needs to be collected from the store every week. The manager of Happyshopper is very keen to recycle and has arranged special collections of the cardboard and plastic to be taken away for recycling every week.

2   Which of the following businesses has a greater environmental impact on the world?

a) Caspian Chemical Company manufactures a range of dangerous chemicals. The rivers and sea near the company's factory in England often have dead fish in them. The company has been in trouble with the Environment Agency.

b) Pluto Pharmaceuticals manufactures a range of drugs for use in hospitals. They are very careful about the chemicals that they use to manufacture the drugs and like to get involved in environmental projects. Recently, they paid for new woodland to be planted near one of their factories in Wales.

Task 1

If possible, work in a small group to carry out this task. Use the Internet to find information about local services that are available for recycling. Make a note of at least five different services and list why you think they would be useful and who might use them. When you have finished this task, your group should be prepared to discuss its findings with the rest of the class.

Recycling service	Why this is useful	Who might use this service

How 'green' can we go?

As well as recycling and being **'green'**, many businesses are also interested in **sustainability**. Sustainability means that we try to replace things that we use up. For example, many things that we use every day are made from wood or trees. How many things can you think of that are made from wood or trees?

A very obvious example is paper. Every day, we use lots of paper in the world and it is made from trees. We can sustain the environment by planting new trees to replace the ones that we cut down to turn into paper and other products.

Can you think of other ways that we can help to sustain the environment? What other things that we use up are replaceable? Make a list or discuss in a group.

What this means

'Being green' a reference that usually means trying to be kind(er) to the environment, for example by recycling.

Recycling making use of things that we have used and will throw away and turning them into something else.

Environmental policy when a business thinks about how the goods and services that it provides impact on the environment.

'Green' a term used to identify something that is kind to the environment.

Sustainability this means trying to replace things that we use up.

Tom is keen to build on the garden centre's 'green' reputation. He thinks a good way to do this is to team up with the local council. He would like to make the garden centre a place that people can bring things to be recycled. If he offers **incentives** to his customers then this may increase their recycling. If he also teams up with the local council, they could promote the garden centre as a place to **recycle** and he may be able to sell some of the materials for recycling back to the council. This could potentially increase the number of customers and level of sales at the garden centre as well as increase money coming in from other sources.

What this means

'Being green' a reference that usually means trying to be kind(er) to the environment, for example by recycling.

Environmental policy when a business thinks about how the goods and services that it provides impact on the environment.

'Green' a term used to identify something that is kind to the environment.

Incentive a free bonus offered to customers in return for doing something.

Recycle/Recycling making use of things that we have used and will throw away and turning them into something else.

Sustainability this means trying to replace things that we use up

Task 2

Tom has asked Alice and Lee to make a list of all the materials that could reasonably be collected at the garden centre for recycling. He suggests that they could use the Internet to research this. He would like two lists to be created: one list for items at the garden centre that should be recycled and another list of items that customers might bring with them to the garden centre for recycling. Create the two lists for them. You may wish to complete this task in a group.

How 'green' can we go?

Task 3

Tom has asked Alice and Lee to produce a poster to advertise the recycling facilities that are available at the garden centre for customers to use and the incentive scheme it is offering. The poster should include the following information which will encourage customers to recycle.

- All customers are encouraged to take part in the recycle scheme.
- Customers can gain 'green' points once they have registered for the Huntingdale Green Scheme.
- All customers start at RED level.
- Customers who complete five visits to the garden centre, make a purchase and deposit items for recycling at the recycling station will progress to AMBER level.
- AMBER level customers are entitled to FREE tea or coffee in the café.
- Customers who complete 10 visits to the garden centre, make a purchase and deposit items for recycling at the recycling station will progress to YELLOW level.
- YELLOW level customers are entitled to a 5% saving on their purchases from the garden centre.
- Customers who complete 20 visits to the garden centre, make a purchase and deposit items for recycling at the recycling station will progress to GREEN level.
- GREEN level customers are entitled to a 10% saving on their purchases from the garden centre.

Make the poster for Alice and Lee.

Links to other subjects

In Geography/Environmental Studies you might learn about the impact business and industry can have on the local environment and how this impact can be reduced by recycling.

Check your learning

1 How might Huntingdale Garden Centre become 'greener'?

Tick all the correct answers.	
Increase pollution	
Increase the amount of recycling	
Use more 'green' products	
Encourage customers to recycle	
Use rainwater to flush the toilets	

2 Think about what goes on in your school that is 'green'. What activities take place to encourage recycling?

3 Think about recycling at home. What kinds of things do you recycle from your house? Do you have different bins for different kinds of rubbish?

4 Why do you think it is important to recycle?

5 Carry out some research using the Internet to find out how different items can be recycled. Write a short report of your findings and email it to your teacher or parent/carer to show what you know about recycling.

If you have time, complete this task in a group and present your findings to the rest of the class.

Complete a Peer Assessment Sheet if you did this task in a group. Complete a Self-assessment Sheet if you did it on your own. The Sheets can be photocopied from the Appendices.

How 'green' can we go?

How can we be enterprising?

Experiences and outcomes covered	SOC 3–20a, SOC 3–21a, TCH 3–06a, TCH 3–07a, TCH 3–07b
Topics covered	Enterprise, ethics, sustainability
Knowledge and skills	Word processing, spreadsheets, charts, numeracy, creative thought, report writing, research, decision making
Resources needed	Access to a computer, word-processing software, spreadsheet software, relevant e-files (see Introduction)

What is enterprise? It's a word that we often hear when people speak about business. Do you know what enterprise means? Take a minute to discuss this with a classmate.

Did you come up with a good definition? If you used a dictionary, you would find that the word enterprise can mean a project or some kind of work. It also refers to something that uses initiative or resourcefulness. If you are not sure of these words, ask your teacher to explain them further.

Sometimes when people talk about enterprise, they also talk about 'entrepreneurs'. Entrepreneurs could be described as enterprising people in business. In other words, they take a business idea and make it work. In economics, we would describe an entrepreneur as someone who brings together different factors in business such as land, labour and capital in such a way that they make the business idea work and generate money.

Think of entrepreneurs that you know in business and discuss these people in a group. What makes these people successful? What qualities do they have in common? Are these the kind of people that you might aspire to be like when you enter the world of work?

Task 1

You can complete this task individually or in a group.

If you have an enterprise group in your school, find out about the work of the group and the businesses they have set up. If you don't have an enterprise group in your school, then think of what such a group might do in your school to be enterprising. Think about the qualities that members of the group would need for it to be successful and list as many as possible. Once you have done this, write down some reasons why the different qualities might make the group a success or a failure!

Task 2

At the start of this ILO you were asked to identify well-known and successful entrepreneurs. Choose one of the people that you identified (or choose a completely new one if you prefer) and research their background and business(es). Write a short report of about 250 words summarising their entrepreneurial skills and their business successes. Try to find out if they contribute anything else to society. For example, do they support charitable causes or do they have a good track record of operating 'green' businesses?

It's worth remembering that we don't need to run a large company and make millions of pounds to be enterprising. Any activity that takes a new business idea and makes it work is enterprising!

Alice and Lee were asked to take part in the **enterprise** group at school. They decided to ask their parents if they could set up a stall at the garden centre to sell the goods that the group produces. Their enterprise business at school designs and manufactures bird houses from **sustainable** materials.

How can we be enterprising?

What this means

Enterprise making a business idea work.

Sustainable using things that can be replaced easily and therefore cause little harm to the environment.

Further information relating to the costs of making the bird houses is available in the file HGC Bird House (a word-processing file; see page 55). Alice and Lee hoped to sell each bird house for £8 and to sell the bird houses on four consecutive Saturdays at the garden centre. First they created a spreadsheet with estimates of sales for the four Saturdays. The spreadsheet file HGC Bird House Sales (see page 56) contains this information. Then after the fourth Saturday, they added the information about the actual sales made over the four Saturdays to the HGC Bird House spreadsheet.

Task 3

Using the e-files available to you, populate the spreadsheet file with the costs and actual sales figures so that you can work out the profit or loss that has been made from making and selling the bird houses.

Task 4

Alice and Lee have also been asked by their enterprise group to create a short report using the information from the spreadsheet. The report should include the following:

- a front cover
- information on the number of bird houses sold
- information on the value (£) of bird houses sold
- the profit or loss that was made.

Tip: it may be useful to show some of this information in the form of charts or graphs.

Create the report for them.

If you completed Tasks 3 and 4 in a group you should now complete a Peer Assessment Sheet. The Sheet can be photocopied from the Appendices.

Links to other subjects

In Accounting you will learn about businesses and how they make money and profits.

In Maths you will learn about money and its management.

In Administration and IT you will learn about using spreadsheets.

Check your learning

1 If an enterprising idea is to be successful, how do you think this would be achieved?

Tick all the correct answers.	
Having a good idea	
Lack of money to make the idea work	
Working hard and taking good advice	
Producing products that people want to buy	
Providing poor customer service	

2 Do you have an enterprise group in your school? If so, write down a list of the things that they are good at doing and the products that they produce or sell. If you don't have an enterprise group at your school, try to find out about any enterprise groups running in your local area.

3 You worked out the profit/loss that the enterprise group made from selling the bird houses. Why do you think it is important for businesses to make a profit?

4 What skills do you think the members of the enterprise group will have learned? List as many as you can.

How can we be enterprising?

What are sustainability and ethics all about?

Experiences and outcomes covered	SOC 3–20a, SOC 3–21a, TCH 3–06a, TCH 3–07a, TCH 3–07b
Topics covered	Enterprise, ethics, sustainability
Knowledge and skills	Word processing, creative thought, report writing, decision making, research
Resources needed	Access to the Internet, word-processing software

Alice and Lee have been asking their parents about how they run their business and how they decide on what products to sell to their customers. Lisa tells Alice and Lee that she carries out a customer survey every year to find out important information about the people who shop at the garden centre. Using the information that she collects, she can decide on the best products to stock and offer for sale. It also allows her to make decisions about how much to stock, what products will be most popular and how much money the customers are likely to spend.

Lisa thinks that a very important aspect of running a successful business is being able to offer **ethical** and **sustainable** products to their customers. Alice and Lee are not sure what the words 'ethical' and 'sustainable' mean.

What this means

Ethical doing business in a fair way that does not harm others.

Sustainable using things that can be replaced easily and therefore cause little harm to the environment.

Task 1

Lisa asks Alice and Lee to research the words *ethical* and *sustainable* and write a short report to show why these **business concepts** are important to the success of any business. Lisa thinks it would be good to show this report to the enterprise group at the school. She also thinks it would be good if Alice and Lee could include the following in the report.

- An example of good business ethics either in general or an example that is found in the course of the research being carried out.

- Examples of sustainable products that might be offered for sale in the garden centre and the benefits of offering them for sale to customers.

Write the report for Alice and Lee.

What this means

Business concepts rules that people use in business.

Links to other subjects

In Business and Business Management you will learn about the importance of marketing to businesses. You will also learn about business ethics.

What are sustainability and ethics all about?

Check your learning

1 Here's a list of things that are used in the garden centre. Which ones are sustainable products?

Tick all the correct answers.	
Paper plates in the café	
Recyclable plant pots	
Plastic cutlery in the café	
Disposable napkins in the café	
Hand driers in the toilets	

2 Discuss with a group of your friends why you think it is important for people in business to be ethical. Share your findings with the rest of the class.

Complete a Peer Assessment Sheet as part of this activity. The Sheet can be photocopied from the Appendices.

How can we help the local community?

Experiences and outcomes covered	TCH 3–02a, SOC 3–21a, TCH 3–06a, TCH 3–07a, TCH 3–07b
Topics covered	Sustainable development
Knowledge and skills	Research, word processing, creative thought, report writing
Resources needed	Access to the Internet, word-processing software

A plastic-bottle greenhouse

Tom and Lisa have been approached by the local primary school and asked to take part in a 'green' project. The details are as follows:

■ The local primary school wishes to build several sustainable greenhouses in which they can grow plants.

■ The greenhouses will be made of recycled plastic bottles attached to a wooden frame.

- The school has been collecting bottles for some time and think that they have enough to build two greenhouses.

The headteacher of the primary school has asked Tom and Lisa for two things:

- a piece of land at the garden centre where they can build the greenhouses
- a donation of some seeds so that the pupils can grow plants.

Tom and Lisa have already marked an area ('the wilderness') on the map of the garden centre to be used to build the greenhouses. This is available to view on page xii and in the file ILO7MAP.JPG

Task 1

Tom and Lisa have agreed to the request although it is clear to them that the teachers don't know much about greenhouses or the plants that they could grow. Tom and Lisa have asked Alice and Lee to produce a report that they can show to the teachers at the school. It requires some research to be carried out and must include the following information:

- details about plastic-bottle greenhouses
- how to build them
- materials required
- maintenance
- advantages over traditional glass greenhouses
- any disadvantages of building and using plastic-bottle greenhouses
- a list of suitable plants that the children could grow in the greenhouses.

Produce the report for Alice and Lee.

This task is best completed as part of a group. When finished, you should complete a Peer Assessment Sheet. The Sheet can be photocopied from the Appendices.

Note: ILO 8 continues and develops the themes from ILO 7.

Can we make money out of being 'green'?

Experiences and outcomes covered	TCH 3–02a, SOC 3–21a, TCH 3–06a, TCH 3–07a, TCH 3–07b
Topics covered	Sustainable development
Knowledge and skills	Research, word processing, spreadsheets, creative thought, report writing
Resources needed	Access to a computer, word-processing software, spreadsheet software, relevant e-file (see Introduction)

There is currently a piece of land at the garden centre which is not used at all. Tom and Lisa have already agreed that the primary school can build two plastic-bottle greenhouses on this piece of land. Alice and Lee call it 'the wilderness' as it is a piece of land belonging to the garden centre that has never been developed. Tom and Lisa have spread wild flower seeds across the area to improve its appearance but do not have any plans to develop it. This is mainly due to the cost of improving it.

Tom has come up with a good idea which could make some extra money for the garden centre. His idea is very simple. He will get some of his own workers to build a

Can we make money out of being 'green'?

What this means

Discount money off something.

Advertising telling people about things you are selling.

'village' of plastic-bottle greenhouses and create a garden community where people can rent a greenhouse plus a patch of garden land 4 m by 3 m. Each person will pay a monthly rent of £20 and they will be able to access their greenhouse and garden patch during normal opening hours. The garden centre will provide water and all customers will be able to claim 15% **discount** on plants and seeds for as long as they rent a greenhouse. Tom has worked out that he can fit 30 greenhouses/garden patches on the piece of land but it will cost him £6000 to get the land in order and have the greenhouses built. He has already asked the café manager to start saving plastic bottles.

Task 1

Tom has asked Alice and Lee to complete the spreadsheet that he has started to fill out using the information that he has provided. The file is called Greenhouses.xls (see page 57). Tom needs the spreadsheet to be completed for Years 1–5. He has worked out these additional costs:

- year 1 **advertising** £500
- years 2–5 advertising £300
- years 2–5 **maintenance costs** £200 per year
- year 3 **expansion** costs (planned construction of five additional greenhouses) £2500 (note that this will change the income for years 4 and 5 as there will be 35 greenhouses/garden patches
- years 1–5 **administration costs** £250 per year.

Tom has asked Alice and Lee to work out the following information and show it on the spreadsheet file:

- the profit or loss for each of years 1–5
- a suitable chart showing the total income and the total expenditure for each year.

Complete the spreadsheet for them.

This task can be completed individually or as part of a group. In either case, a Peer or Self-assessment Sheet should be completed as appropriate. The Sheets can be photocopied from the Appendices.

What this means

Maintenance costs the costs of keeping things working.

Expansion growing the business.

Administration costs the costs of keeping the business running.

Task 2

Tom has asked Alice and Lee to produce an advertising poster that can be put up at the garden centre to give people details about the new greenhouses/garden patches. It must include all of the relevant information, including costs.

Produce the poster for them.

What this means

Administration costs the costs of keeping the business running.

Advertising telling people about things you are selling.

Discount money off something.

Expansion growing the business.

Maintenance costs the costs of keeping things working.

Links to other subjects

In Accounting and Business Management you will learn about how different businesses grow and develop.

In Administration and IT you will learn how to use spreadsheet software to do calculations and make charts and graphs.

Check your learning

1 Match each word a–e with the correct description i–v.

   a) expansion
   b) administration
   c) profit
   d) discount
   e) maintenance

   i) costs of running a business
   ii) money you make in business
   iii) growing the business
   iv) costs of keeping things working
   v) money off

2 Why might the garden centre offer a discount?

3 How could Tom reduce the advertising costs?

4 How could Tom reduce the maintenance costs?

5 Would Tom prefer to make a profit or a loss? Explain your answer.

6 Give a reason why customers may be interested in renting a greenhouse/garden patch.

Can we make money out of being 'green'?

Technology development

Experiences and outcomes covered	TCH 3–08a, TCH 3–07b
Topics covered	The Internet, online safety, technological developments
Knowledge and skills	Presenting information, team working, technology development
Resources needed	Access to the Internet, word-processing software

We live in a world where technology is all around us and we probably use technology every day without even realising it. Businesses use technology as part of their day-to-day activities. It can be used for making products, for planning and organising events and for communicating with other people.

For example, Huntingdale Garden Centre has a website. Websites can be used to give customers information about products for sale and some can even allow customers to buy goods online. This is known as **electronic commerce** or **e-commerce**. To be able to access a website you need to have a website address which is known as a **URL – uniform resource locator**.

A URL might look like this: **http://www.google.com**

You also need to have a modem and a telephone line. A **modem** links a computer to the telephone line which then connects to the Internet. Many businesses now use an Internet connection that is fast – this is known as **broadband**.

What this means

E-commerce buying and selling products on the Internet.

URL (uniform resource locator) a website address.

Modem links a computer to the Internet through a telephone line.

Broadband a special type of Internet connection that is fast.

There are advantages and disadvantages of having a website for a business:

Advantages	Disadvantages
■ Customers can buy goods online 24 hours a day	■ Can be expensive to buy and maintain a website
■ The business doesn't need to have shops to sell goods	■ Staff need to be shown how to use the website and this training can be expensive

CLICK CEOP
Internet Safety

The Child Exploitation and Online Protection Centre (CEOP) works across the UK tackling child sex abuse and providing advice for parents and young people about staying safe online

People have to be very careful when using the Internet as it can be unsafe. Some information on the Internet can be wrong, and if you are talking to someone over the Internet always remember that they might not be the person they say they are.

Never:

■ tell people where you live or what school you go to

■ give out your mobile phone number

■ arrange to meet someone who you have met over the Internet

■ believe everything that you hear from people online.

Always tell an adult if think something is wrong or are being asked for information that you don't think someone should be asking you. Keep yourself safe!

Technology development

Technology changes!

Technology changes very quickly and it can be hard to keep up to date with the latest gadgets. Here are some examples:

Mobile phone 	**Mobile phones** allow people to talk when they are on the move. Mobiles allow people to send text messages, access the Internet and to carry out lots of different activities. Some mobile phones – 'smartphones' – have different 'apps' that can perform a large number of tasks. Businesses can have their own app to advertise their products and enable people to buy them.
Laptop computer 	A **laptop computer** is a smaller version of a normal computer that sits on a desk. It can be carried around and is often used by people who don't always work in an office.
Tablet computer 	A **tablet computer** such as an iPad™ is a very lightweight and portable computer. It is bigger than a mobile phone but smaller than a laptop computer. It uses **touch-screen technology** to work: people use their fingers to move around the screen. There is no need for a keyboard or a mouse.
WiFi 	**WiFi** allows people to connect to the Internet without the need for cables. Many businesses allow their customers to access WiFi in their shop or restaurant. To be able to use WiFi you need to have a computer or mobile phone that has a wireless facility.

Technology development

Social networking	**Social networking** has become very popular. Many people now use websites such as Facebook and Twitter to keep in touch with their friends. People can post information about themselves, videos, photographs and other information. Businesses can use social networking to let customers know about new products or events.
	Remember to be careful on social networking sites – they can be dangerous.
Wiki	A **Wiki** is a website that anyone can edit. This means anyone can add more information, change information or even delete it.
Blog	A **blog** is like an online diary that people use to record what is happening in their life. They might write about what has been going on that day.
3-D television	Being able to watch something in 3-D was limited to the cinema for a number of years. However, people can now have **3-D television** in their own homes. 3-D TV makes people think that items and objects are coming out of the screen! You need to wear 3-D glasses so that you can watch 3-D TV properly.

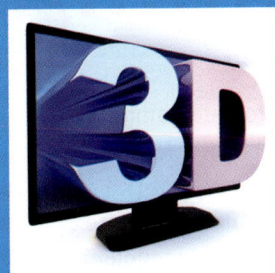

What this means

Mobile phone a portable telephone.

Laptop computer a small computer that is portable.

Tablet computer a computer smaller than a laptop that does not have a separate keyboard.

Touch-screen technology a special screen that requires the user to use their finger to move around it.

WiFi connecting to the Internet without cables.

Social networking site a website that allows people to keep in touch with others by posting messages and updates.

Wiki a website that can be edited or changed by any user.

Blog an online diary that details what someone has been doing.

3-D television a special TV that allows you to see objects in three dimensions.

Task 1

Prepare a poster that has five golden rules for keeping safe when using the Internet.

Task 2

This task is designed to be carried out as a class. You are going to set up a class wiki that tells people all about technological developments. Your teacher will put you into small groups of two or three and give each group a technological development to write about. On the wiki, each group should write about their technological development and some of its advantages and disadvantages. Other members of the class will be able to see this and can add more information to the wiki. By the end of the task, the class will have produced a wiki full of information about technology development.

Now complete a Peer Assessment Sheet. The Sheet can be photocopied from the Appendices.

Task 3

Access this website: **www.bbc.co.uk/webwise/**.

It has lots of different information and tasks about using the Internet and social networking. Spend some time reading the information, making some notes about what you learn and carrying out the different tasks.

What this means

Blog an online diary that details what someone has been doing.

Broadband a special type of Internet connection that is fast.

E-commerce buying and selling products on the Internet.

Laptop computer a small computer that is portable.

Mobile phone a portable telephone.

Modem links a computer to the Internet through a telephone line.

Social networking site a website that allows people to keep in touch with others by posting messages and updates.

Tablet computer a computer smaller than a laptop that does not have a separate keyboard.

Touch-screen technology a special screen that requires the user to use their finger to move around it.

URL (uniform resource locator) a website address.

WiFi connecting to the Internet without cables.

Wiki a website that can be edited or changed by any user.

3-D television a special TV that allows you to see objects in three dimensions.

Links to other subjects

You will learn about technology development in lots of subjects. Different subjects will use different technologies for different purposes.

Check your learning

1 Match each word a–e with the correct description i–v.

a) WiFi

b) wiki

c) blog

d) laptop computer

e) tablet computer

i) a computer smaller than a laptop that does not have a separate keyboard.

ii) an online diary that details what someone has been doing.

iii) a small computer that is portable.

iv) a website that can be edited or changed by the user.

v) connecting to the Internet without cables.

2 Why might a business like Huntingdale Garden Centre use the Internet?

Tick all the correct answers.	
To advertise their products	
To sell goods online	
To find out what the competition is doing	
To create a social networking site	
To transport goods to their customers	

3 Give two examples of what Huntingdale Garden Centre could use a social networking site for.

4 Some mobile phones are 'smart'. What do smartphones have that ordinary phones don't have?

5 What do you use to find your way around a touch screen?

6 What do you need to have to connect to the Internet?

Tick all the correct answers.	
Modem	
Speakers	
Computer	
Telephone line	
Printer	

7 Answer the following questions by writing true or false next to each one.

a) A website that you can edit and change is known as a blog.

b) Broadband is a type of Internet connection that is fast.

c) You need cables to be able to use WIFI.

d) You can access the Internet through a mobile phone.

e) People don't always tell the truth on the Internet.

f) Facebook is an example of a social network.

g) A website address is known as a uniform resource locator (URL).

h) A tablet computer and a laptop computer are the same thing.

i) Technology can be used when planning and organising events.

Using technology to reach our customers

Experiences and outcomes covered	TCH 3-03a, TCH 3-04a, TCH 3-06a, TCH 3-07b
Topics covered	Use of word processing and databases
Knowledge and skills	Word processing, database, creative thought, writing skills
Resources needed	Access to a computer, word-processing software, database software, appropriate e-file (see Introduction)

This ILO can be carried out individually or as a group.

Many businesses make use of technology to run the business and keep in touch with their customers. Mobile technology, sometimes called 'M' technology, allows communication to take place while people are on the go. Perhaps you have a mobile phone. If so, you are making use of M technology. The use of M technology in business means that business can take place all over the world at any time.

The most common uses of M technology are:

- sending short messages by text (SMS)
- sending and receiving photographs
- sending and receiving **email**
- accessing the Internet.

What this means

Email electronic mail sent from a computer using an email address.

Businesses need equipment to carry out their day-to-day activities. The most common pieces of equipment found in modern business are shown in the table on the following pages.

Photocopier	A **photocopier** is used to make multiple copies of documents. It can perform different functions such as printing double-sided and reducing or enlarging the document to be copied.
Scanner	A **scanner** is used to make an electronic copy of a document. It is usually attached to a computer.
Printer	A **printer** is used to produce a 'hard' (paper) copy of an electronic document. It could be attached to a computer or a network of computers.
Multi-function device (MFD)	A **multi-function device** is a machine that combines the functions of a printer, scanner and photocopier. It is a popular choice in modern offices as it does the work of three different machines without needing space for the separate machines. These devices are also very reasonably priced.

Using technology to reach our customers

Smartphone	A **smartphone** is a mobile phone which has many computing functions built in to it. Apple and Blackberry are popular manufacturers of these products.
Notebook/netbook/laptop	A **notebook**, **netbook** or **laptop** is an alternative to a desktop computer. They each have the advantage of being small and portable.

Virtually all businesses use computers. Computers are only useful when there is software available to carry out the tasks of the business. The most common software used in business today includes:

Word-processing software	**Word-processing** software is used to present and communicate written information. This could be used to send letters to customers.
Spreadsheet software	A **spreadsheet** is used to store, edit and arrange numbers. Many businesses use this software to present and store financial information. It can also be used to create graphs and charts.
Database software	A **database** is used to store information and records. It is good for storing information about customers.
Presentation software	**Presentation** software is used to create electronic presentations for an audience.
Desktop publishing software	**Desktop publishing** software is used to create posters, adverts, company newsletters etc.

Using technology to reach our customers

Workstation assessment

Before using a computer at work or home, it is good practice to carry out a workstation assessment. This is used to assess various aspects of your working environment which should be appropriate for the work that you are carrying out. It includes an assessment of the following:

- desk
- chair
- computer screen
- keyboard
- space
- environment.

You should now carry out a workstation assessment of your work area. Your teacher will be able to provide you with a checklist to complete (the photocopiable form can be found in the Appendices).

Lisa is keen to keep in touch with customers who are loyal to the garden centre. Many businesses make use of modern technology to keep in touch with their customers. This can be to inform them of special offers in order to encourage them to visit and make a purchase. Businesses may also use customers' email addresses to send them information. This might be to tell them about a special event taking place or to tell them about a new line of stock.

All of the following tasks can be completed individually or as part of a group. In either case, you should complete a Peer or Self-assessment Sheet when you have completed the tasks. (The Peer and Self-assessment Sheets can be photocopied from the Appendices.)

Task 1

Working in a small group or by yourself, write down the names of at least three different pieces of technology or software that a business might use. Now make a list of five things that each piece of technology or software could be used for in business. Present your ideas to the rest of the class.

What this means

Recycling making use of things that we have used and will throw away and turning them into something else.

The staff at Huntingdale Garden Centre have already started to populate a database with customer information collected when people register for the garden centre's **recycling** scheme. This information is contained in the file CustomerDatabase (see pages 58–59). Before you start the next task, discuss with your classmates the advantages to the garden centre of using a database to store information.

Task 2

The information in the table on the following page needs to be added to the database. It relates to the 'recycle level' that has been allocated to each customer – red, amber, yellow or green. Create a new field in the database for the 'Recycle level' and update the CustomerDatabase file with this information.

Using technology to reach our customers

Customer number	Recycle level	Customer number	Recycle level	Customer number	Recycle level
1	Amber	11	Yellow	21	Yellow
2	Red	12	Yellow	22	Red
3	Green	13	Amber	23	Amber
4	Amber	14	Green	24	Amber
5	Amber	15	Red	25	Amber
6	Red	16	Red	26	Red
7	Red	17	Red	27	Red
8	Red	18	Amber	28	Red
9	Yellow	19	Yellow	29	Amber
10	Red	20	Yellow	30	Red

Task 3

Lisa has decided that in order to save money she will only contact customers by email. However, some customers have not provided an email address. The information will need to be posted to customers who have not supplied an email address. Lisa has started work on an information sheet about the latest special offers at the garden centre and this has to be sent out to all customers.

Your task is to produce a mail merge for customers in the database who have not supplied an email address and use the information sheet file (Information.doc; see page 60) to complete this task. Print out one copy of the merge document and the first merged file to show that you have completed this task successfully.

What this means

Email electronic mail sent from a computer using an email address.

Recycling making use of things that we have used and will throw away and turning them into something else.

Task 4

Alice and Lee suggested to their Mum that it would be a good idea to send an email to customers in the database with a flyer advertising special events at the garden centre. In the coming months, Tom and Lisa have planned the following:

- A visit by the celebrity gardener Alan Greenfinger on 5 June at 10am.
- A talk by the famous gardening writer, author of the bestselling book *Herbs and Flowers for All*, Margaret Sage-Parsley on 20 June at 2pm.
- Strawberries and cream served in the café throughout the month of June.
- Free bouncy castle for children every weekend in June.

Prepare a flyer to advertise these special events. Print out a copy if you are able to do so.

Use the CustomerDatabase file to create a distribution list of customers who can be emailed a copy of the flyer. Print out one copy of this distribution list.

Links to other subjects

In Business Management you will learn about marketing and how businesses contact and attract customers.

In Administration & IT you will learn how to use business software that is useful to the smooth running of a business.

Check your learning

1 Match each word a–e with the correct description i–v.
   a) word processing
   b) spreadsheet
   c) database
   d) PowerPoint
   e) web browser

   i)   used to store records
   ii) used to produce written documents
   iii) used to create presentations
   iv) used to find information on the Internet
   v)   used for calculations

2 Why might the garden centre wish to contact customers?

3 How could Lisa save money when getting in touch with customers?

4 List some additional information that the garden centre may wish to collect from its customers and store in the database.

Using technology to reach our customers

Huntingdale Garden Centre Project File: HGC Sales

Projected sales and costs from January–December this year

	Jan	Feb	Mar	Apr	May	Jun	Jul	Aug	Sep	Oct	Nov	Dec
Sales (£)	15000	18000	27000	36000	49000	68000	67000	72000	55000	44000	45000	22000
Costs (£)	18000	18000	22000	21000	32000	44000	43000	46000	33000	28000	29000	18000

Notes:

- £25000 is payable in April this year for the new car park.
- Sales for February onwards this year are estimated.

Sales from last year

	Jan	Feb	Mar	Apr	May	Jun	Jul	Aug	Sep	Oct	Nov	Dec
Sales (£)	26000	28000	25000	33000	47000	60000	60000	65000	50000	40000	37000	18000

© Hodder & Stoughton Limited 2012. Copying permitted in the purchasing institution only.

Profit/loss forecast for this year Project File: HGC Forecast

	Jan	Feb	Mar	Apr	May	Jun	Jul	Aug	Sept	Oct	Nov	Dec	TOTALS
Sales													
Costs													
Additional costs													
TOTALS													

© Hodder & Stoughton Limited 2012. Copying permitted in the purchasing institution only.

Profit made in January Project File: HGC Profit

	Unit cost (£)	Unit selling price (£)	Profit per unit (£)	Quantity sold	Total profit (£)
Christmas tree (1 metre)	5	10		200	
Christmas tree (2 metres)	6	12		145	
Christmas pudding (500g)	0.8	2		60	
Christmas pudding (1kg)	1.75	3.5		80	
Bunch of Christmas flowers (small)	1.75	4		240	
Bunch of Christmas flowers (large)	2.5	6		280	
Fairtrade Christmas chocolate (400g)	1.25	3		65	
Fairtrade Christmas chocolate (1kg)	2	5		45	

© Hodder & Stoughton Limited 2012. Copying permitted in the purchasing institution only.

Bird House Project File: HGC Bird House

Huntingdale Garden Centre Bird House Project

Cost of materials to make **one** bird house – £2.00

Cost of paint to decorate **one** bird house – £1.00

Other costs associated with making **one** bird house – £1.00

Total cost of making **one** bird house – £?

Selling price of **one** bird house – £8.00

Actual bird house sales:

1st Saturday	15
2nd Saturday	25
3rd Saturday	37
4th Saturday	22

© Hodder & Stoughton Limited 2012. Copying permitted in the purchasing institution only.

Appendices

Bird House Project File: HGC Bird House Sales

	1st Saturday	2nd Saturday	3rd Saturday	4th Saturday
ESTIMATED bird house sales	10	25	30	35
Value of bird house sales (£)				
Cost of bird house sales (£)				
Profit/(Loss)				
ACTUAL bird house sales				
Value of bird house sales (£)				
Cost of bird house sales (£)				
Profit/(Loss)				
SELLING PRICE PER BIRD HOUSE (£)				
COSTS PER BIRD HOUSE (£)				

© Hodder & Stoughton Limited 2012. Copying permitted in the purchasing institution only.

Plastic-bottle Greenhouse Project File: Greenhouses

	Year 1	Year 2	Year 3	Year 4	Year 5
MONEY IN					
Rent received from greenhouses/ garden patches					
MONEY OUT					
Set up costs for Year 1					
Advertising					
Maintenance costs					
Expansion costs					
Administration costs					
PROFIT or LOSS PER YEAR					

© Hodder & Stoughton Limited 2012. Copying permitted in the purchasing institution only.

Recycle Level Project File: CustomerDatabase

Customer number	Title	Firstname	Surname	Address	Town/City	Postcode	Email address
1	Mr	Colin	Murray	22 Rose Wynd	North Berwick	EH39 8GH	c.murray@me.com
2	Miss	Ruth	Handle	54 High View Street	North Berwick	EH39 2PJ	handles@plusnet.net
3	Mr	Robert	Winters	39 Fisher Crescent	North Berwick	EH39 6TF	bobwinters@coolmail.net
4	Mrs	Hetty	Humphreys	2 Golden View Road	Edinburgh	EH4 8TH	hetty@humphreys.com
5	Miss	Hannah	Smith	3 Baillie Terrace	Edinburgh	EH6 2CD	
6	Mr	Hugh	Arundel	4 Sea Street	North Berwick	EH39 2QS	harundel@plusmail.co.uk
7	Mrs	Carol	Cuthbert	80 Low Drive	North Berwick	EH39 3PL	carol76@mobilemail.com
8	Mrs	Morag	Mathieson	6 The Terraces	North Berwick	EH39 5HW	moragmath@mymail.co.uk
9	Mr	Jonathan	Lees	34 Crosstrees Place	North Berwick	EH39 1SD	jonnylees@123.com
10	Mr	Dave	Newman	55 Saughton Place	Edinburgh	EH5 8NB	
11	Miss	Marina	Brown	32a Hope Street	North Berwick	EH39 1RT	
12	Miss	Sadie	Musgrove	112 Windyhill Road	North Berwick	EH39 9XA	musgroves@mail4me.com
13	Mr	Stuart	Stevens	120 North Street	North Berwick	EH39 4FD	stueystevens@eeemail.com
14	Mrs	Irene	Perret	9 The Gables	North Berwick	EH39 7QT	perreti33@fastmail.co.uk
15	Mrs	Margaret	Boyd	1b Cleaner Close	North Berwick	EH39 7LM	margaret.boyd@mymail.com

© Hodder & Stoughton Limited 2012. Copying permitted in the purchasing institution only.

Customer number	Title	Firstname	Surname	Address	Town/City	Postcode	Email address
16	Mr	Craig	Bannerman	49 Eastpark Avenue	Edinburgh	EH8 8TT	banners@fastmail.co.uk
17	Mr	William	Stewart	8 Mansion Park	Edinburgh	EH3 2RD	willstewart@plusnet.net
18	Mr	Gary	Williams	2 New Street	North Berwick	EH39 2TU	gary334@1mail1.com
19	Miss	Veronica	Curran	9 Treetop Circle	North Berwick	EH39 3BB	
20	Mrs	Yvette	Fisher	86 Alderly Avenue	Edinburgh	EH6 3GH	fishyfishy@mymail.com
21	Mrs	Janie	Frew	123 Haze Avenue	North Berwick	EH39 9LK	frewtheshrew@freemail.com
22	Mr	Malcolm	Montgomery	1 Wishbone Drive	North Berwick	EH39 2DS	monty88@coolmail.net
23	Mr	Mark	Courtney	44 Washburn Drive	North Berwick	EH39 5NJ	courts997@plusmail.co.uk
24	Miss	Barbara	Johnson	3 Fairview Way	North Berwick	EH39 3JK	babs65@greatmail.com
25	Mrs	Nanette	Anderson	87 Greystone Place	North Berwick	EH39 8XK	n.anderson@mobilemail.com
26	Mr	Abdul	Anwar	265 Long Road	Edinburgh	EH6 7CD	theanwars@fastmail.co.uk
27	Miss	Katie	Cheung	10 Golf Drive	North Berwick	EH39 9EF	katiecheung@me.com
28	Mr	Norman	Webster	Ivy Cottage	North Berwick	EH39 1FS	norman@ivycottage.co.uk
29	Mr	Alan	McNee	78 Turning Circle	North Berwick	EH39 4RP	
30	Mrs	Mary	McDonald	99 Green Street	North Berwick	EH39 8SP	marymac@mymail.com

Appendices

© Hodder & Stoughton Limited 2012. Copying permitted in the purchasing institution only.

Spring Update Project File: Information

Huntingdale Garden Centre

Information Update – Spring

Customer Name

Customer Address

Customer Address

Customer Postcode

Dear Customer

Welcome to the latest update from Huntingdale Garden Centre – your local family garden centre that meets all your gardening needs.

Now that spring is with us, your thoughts will be turning towards sprucing up your garden. We have some great offers that will help you make a good start on tidying up your garden and making it look attractive for the summer months.

Firstly, there is a promotion on all spring plants and flowers, saving 10% on full price. Landscaping products have 15% saving and there are also special meal deals available in the café. All of these promotions run until 15 May.

Remember that as a registered member of our recycle scheme, you can achieve further discounts depending on your 'recycle level'. Recycle as much as you can to work your way up the levels and earn bigger discounts!

We look forward to seeing you in the garden centre soon!

Kind regards

Tom and Lisa

© Hodder & Stoughton Limited 2012. Copying permitted in the purchasing institution only.

Appendices

Workstation Assessment Sheet

Name		Date of assessment

Equipment display screen assessment	Yes ✓	No ✓
Is the display screen image clear?		
Are the characters readable?		
Is the image free of flicker and movement?		
Is the brightness and/or contrast adjustable?		
Does the screen swivel and tilt?		
Is the screen free of glare and reflection?		

Equipment keyboard assessment	Yes ✓	No ✓
Can you tilt the keyboard?		
Is there enough space to rest hands in front of keyboard?		
Is the keyboard comfortable to use?		
Can you find a comfortable keying position?		
Is the keyboard glare free?		
Are the characters on the keys easily readable?		

Equipment work desk assessment	Yes ✓	No ✓
Does the furniture fit the work and the user?		
Is the work surface large enough for documents, keyboard etc.?		
Is there adequate space for you to adopt a comfortable position?		
Is the surface free of glare and reflections?		
Is a document holder provided?		

Equipment work chair assessment	Yes ✓	No ✓
Is the chair stable and does it have easy freedom of movement?		
Is it possible to adjust the backrest (height and tilt), the chair height, and the seat tilt?		
Is your chair comfortable?		
Is a footrest required?		

Appendices

Workstation Assessment Sheet continued

Environment space assessment	Yes ✓	No ✓
Is there enough room to change positions and vary movement?		
Are there any obstructions nearby?		

Environment assessment	Yes ✓	No ✓
Are the levels of light, noise and heat comfortable?		
Is there appropriate adjustable lighting?		
Are the light fittings free from glare?		
Does heat given off from workstation equipment cause the user any discomfort?		
Does any noise pollution from the VDU distract or discomfort the user?		

© Hodder & Stoughton Limited 2012. Copying permitted in the purchasing institution only.

Peer Assessment Sheet

Name of group:

Checklist questions	Yes ✓	No ✓
Did everyone in the group participate?		
Did the group finish their task on time?		
Did the group follow all instructions?		
Did the group ask for help when they got stuck?		
Did everyone in the group come up with ideas?		
Does my teacher think our group worked well?		

Two stars and a wish

Two things we did well:

1

2

One thing next time we need to improve on:

1

Overall, the group would rate their performance as (tick or circle):

Gold　　**Silver**　　**Bronze**

© Hodder & Stoughton Limited 2012. Copying permitted in the purchasing institution only.

Appendices

Self-assessment Sheet

Name of group:

Checklist questions	Yes ✓	No ✓
Did I participate in the task?		
Did I complete everything that was asked of me to the best of my ability?		
Did I complete everything on time?		
Did I contribute ideas in group discussions?		
Did I listen to the views of other people in group discussions?		
Would the other people in my group think that I worked well?		

Two stars and a wish

Two things I did well:

1

2

One thing next time I need to improve on:

1

Overall, I would rate my performance as (tick or circle):

Gold

Silver

Bronze

© Hodder & Stoughton Limited 2012. Copying permitted in the purchasing institution only.

Appendices

Integrated Learning Objects (ILOs) mapping grid

Links to Social Studies and Technologies outcomes

	SOC 3–11a	SOC 3–20a	SOC 3–20b	SOC 3–21a	TCH 3–02a	TCH 3–03a	TCH 3–04a	TCH 3–06a	TCH 3–07a	TCH 3–07b	TCH 3–08a
ILO 1	✓						✓			✓	
ILO 2										✓	
ILO 3		✓	✓	✓		✓	✓	✓	✓	✓	
ILO 4								✓	✓		
ILO 5		✓		✓				✓	✓	✓	
ILO 6		✓		✓				✓	✓	✓	
ILO 7				✓	✓			✓	✓	✓	
ILO 8				✓	✓			✓	✓	✓	
ILO 9										✓	✓
ILO 10						✓	✓	✓		✓	

© Hodder & Stoughton Limited 2012. Copying permitted in the purchasing institution only.

Integrated Learning Objects (ILOs) mapping grid

Links to Literacy, Numeracy and Health and Wellbeing outcomes

© Hodder & Stoughton Limited 2012. Copying permitted in the purchasing institution only.

Index